Maybe YOU need a bath!

Life is so short. Why waste it on unimportant things?

amaze myself...

The unknown stresses me out, dude.

To: _____

Because: _____
_____

Everybody knows that puppies need plenty of sunshine and water!

C'mon! What's five minutes in the grand scheme of things!?

I never get to do anything!

Hey, I've got an idea. Let's play "Drive the Bus"!

UNION SQUARE & CO.
NEW YORK

UNION SQUARE & CO. and the distinctive Union Square & Co. logo
are trademarks of Sterling Publishing Co., Inc.

Union Square & Co., LLC, is a subsidiary of Sterling Publishing Co., Inc.

Text and illustrations © 2023 Mo Willems
A Specific House book.

For information about custom editions, special sales, and premium purchases, please contact
specialsales@unionsquareandco.com.

Printed in the United States of America
10 9 8 7 6 5 4 3 2

unionsquareandco.com

Design by Scott Sosebee

This book is set in Superclarendon, Avenir Pro, Futura Condensed ExtraBold, Tangier, and
The Pigeon Font, with additional handlettering by Mo Willems.
Candy box: Oksanita/iStock/Getty Images Plus

ISBN 978-1-4549-4819-3

Library of Congress Control Number: 2022034228

Be
THE
Bus

The Lost & Profound Wisdom of
The Pigeon
as told to
Mo Willems
with an introduction by
The Bus Driver

UNION
SQUARE
& CO.

NEW YORK

Dear Reader,

Are questions more interesting than answers? **Yes.**

In my capacity as Bus Driver, I am often asked, "What is the best stop for the city center?" or, "What took you so long?" but also, "WHY can't The Pigeon drive the bus?"

It is a question that echoes through the ages like the long, loud honk of a horn being leaned on too enthusiastically by an irresponsible blue bird. The answers are many and almost philosophical in their complexity as they touch upon issues of safety, insurance, proper licensing, union requirements, and, of course, feet being able to reach the pedals.

It turns out, The Pigeon has developed other deep-seated passions over the years, including amassing a collection of short aphorisms, which he calls "peckings of a bird brain."
Here, for the last time ever, are The Pigeon's uncarefully curated thoughts on wisdom, humility, happiness, friendship, love, life, and bus driving.
Making all local stops,
The Bus Driver

Let me be the first to say that everything has already been said.

Like Plato already said,

"Never trust a quotation."

I AM NOT

susceptible to flattery.*

*Unless it's about me.

Genius is seldom recognized.

THAT is why I wear a name tag.

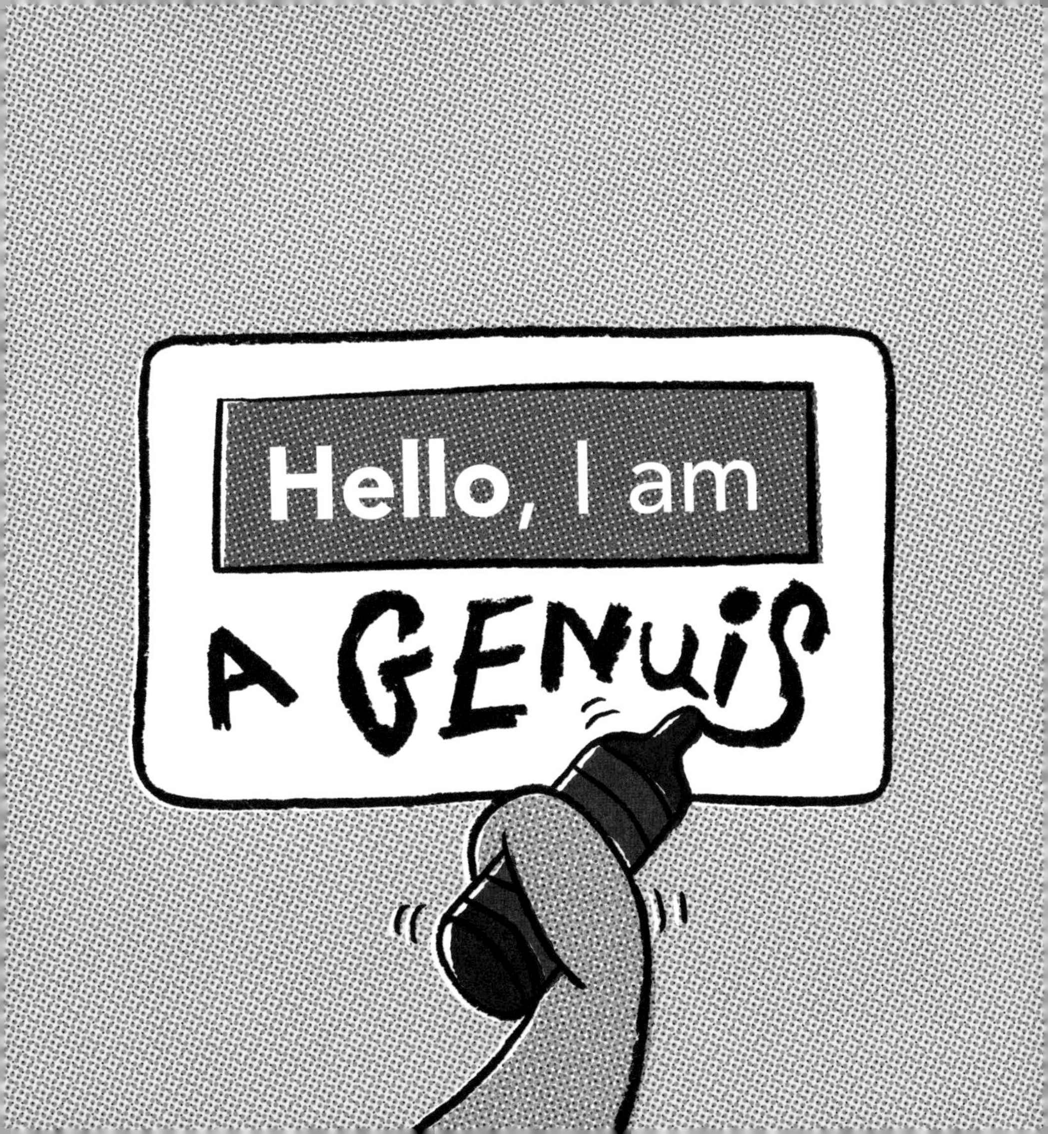
Hello, I am
A GENUIS

NEVER
ever, ever, ever, ever,
ever, ever, ever, ever
GIVE UP!

. . . for at least a month or so.

PRETEND
you have an active imagination.

DRIVE!
like no one is watching.

HONK!
like no one is listening.

DREAM!
like no one is thwarting.

BE
the bus.

WROO

Who figured out that ignorance is bliss

Success is 99% perspiration—

and 5% approximation.

The early bird gets the worm.

NOW do you get why I sleep in?

Dropped food
is gravity's
way of sharing.

I regret nothing—

except that last half a hot dog.

There is a simple solution to not always finding things in the last place you look:

KEEP LOOKING.

"**I**nstant
gratification"
takes
so
loooooooooonngg
to
say.

Aren't
complainers
the WORST?

Surprises

happen when you least expect them.

Happiness is...

escaping a
warm puppy.

Friendship is like riding a bike.

(There's always a chance you'll be grievously injured.)

It is better to give than to receive.

BARELY!

Also, better to say:

"I love you more than ever."

than

"I used to love you less."

Also-also, better to say:

"You are one in a million."

than

"There are 7,960 others just like you out there."

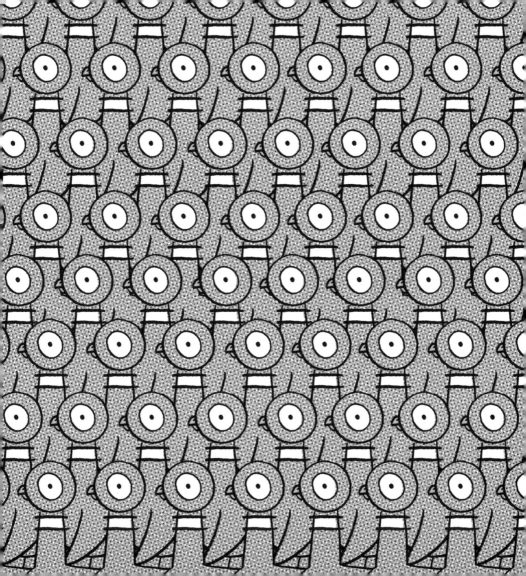

Because you only get one chance to make a twenty-third impression.

Sometimes, I take a good hard look at myself and ask . . .

Wait. Has that weird little bump always been there?

Teachers
and
Librarians

are too brilliant & lovely &
insightful & kind &
effervescent & devoted &
joyful to EVER be
pandered to.

By the way, I think it is perfectly
acceptable to compare apples and oranges.

They are both
fruits of similar shape!

Can be served in slices!!

Available for similar
yet different prices!!!

THEY BOTH JUICE!!!!

In fact,
I WILL go on!

THEY GROW ON TREES!!

Have little stickers on them!!!

OH! They are also about the size of baseballs OR SOMETIMES EVEN SOFTBALLS!!!!

Readily available!!!!! Healthy snacks!!!!!!

Can spit out the seeds!!!!!!!

EASY TO

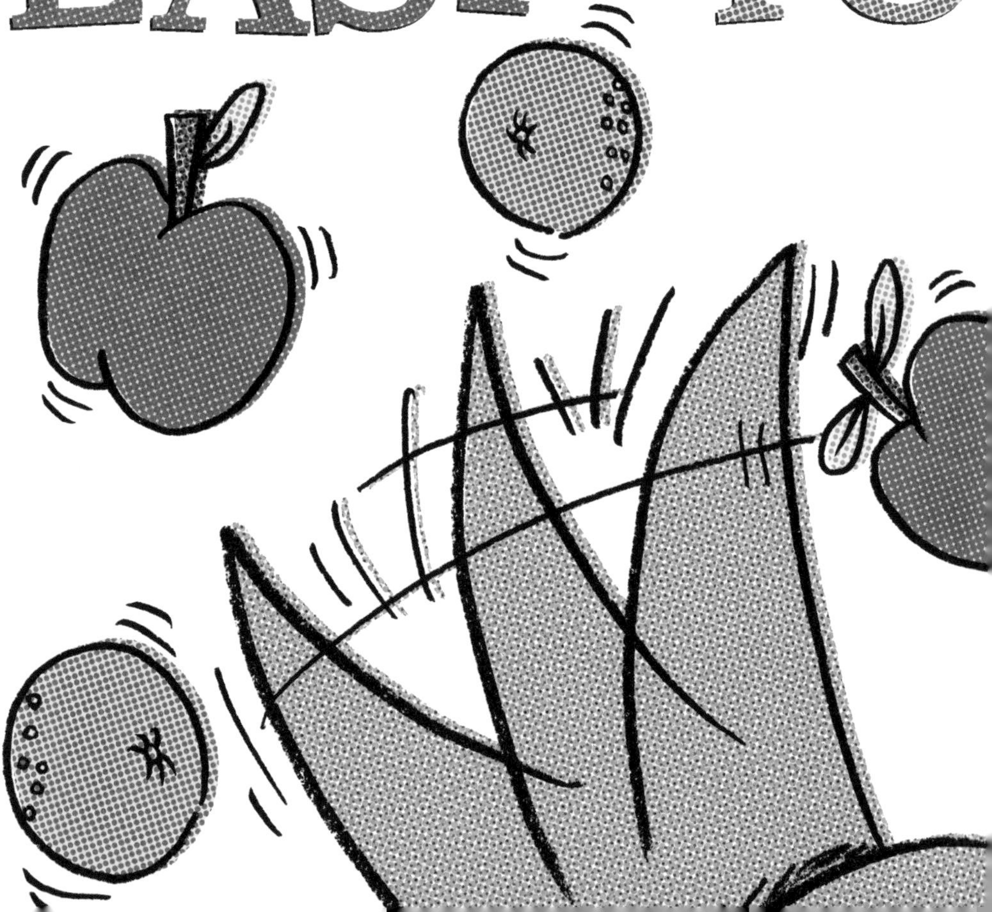

You don't get me.

You can't spell TEAM without ME.

But then you have that TA left over.

LISTEN
to your heart.

FOLLOW
your gut.

WATCH
your step.

If I could change just ONE thing about myself,

I'd be perfect.

Every journey ends by not taking another step.

That's all I got.

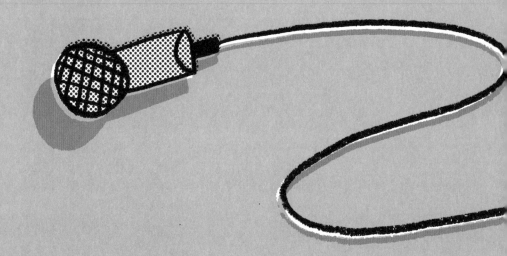

"Other Books"

The Pigeon plans to write someday . . .

You're Okay, I'm Awesome

Pigeons: *America's Most Misunderstood Birds*

Zen and the Art of Bus Maintenance

Pigeon-Whole Yourself: *How to Become
a Thing with Feathers*

Speed: *An Analysis of Cinema's
Greatest Achievement*

One Big I: *How I See Myself*

Bring Hot Dogs!: *Party Planning Made Simple*

How to Take a Train to Escape Your Puppy

The 7 Habits of Highly Effective Bus Drivers

HONK! *And Other Poems*

But, I will demonstrate exemplary patience!
MINE! MINE! MINE!
Ducklings get *everything*!
Y' know, we never get to talk anymore.
If you've never experienced the splendor of a hot dog, you should really...
You just don't understand.
The time is now!
Each morsel is a joy! A celebration in a bun!
Everyone always tells me what to do!
Hubba-Whaa?!?
"Finders, keepers,"